PITTSBURG
P9-EJI-574

OUR PEOPLE

ALSO BY ANGELA SHELF MEDEARIS

Come This Far to Freedom:
A History of African Americans

OUR PEOPLE

by ANGELA SHELF MEDEARIS
illustrated by MICHAEL BRYANT

ATHENEUM 1994 NEW YORK

Maxwell Macmillan Canada
Toronto
Maxwell Macmillan International
New York Oxford Singapore Sydney

Atheneum
Macmillan Publishing Company
866 Third Avenue
New York, NY 10022

Maxwell Macmillan Canada, Inc.
1200 Eglinton Avenue East
Suite 200
Don Mills, Ontario M3C 3N1

Macmillan Publishing Company is part of the Maxwell Communication Group of Companies.

First edition

Printed in Hong Kong by South China Printing Company (1988) Ltd.

10 9 8 7 6 5 4 3 2 1

The text of this book is set in Bembo.

Library of Congress Cataloging-in-Publication Data

Medearis, Angela Shelf, 1956–
Our people / by Angela Shelf Medearis ; illustrated by Michael Bryant. — 1st ed.
p. cm.
Summary: Parent and child discuss their African-American heritage and the contributions made to civilization by their people.
ISBN 0–689–31826–X
1. Afro-Americans—History—Juvenile literature. [1. Afro-Americans—History.] I. Bryant, Michael, ill. II. Title.
E185.M383 1994
973′.04973—dc20 92–44499

For my father—Howard L. Shelf
with love

—A.S.M.

In memory of my mother,
Vera Ellen Bryant,
who made this book possible

—M.B.

Daddy says our people built the pyramids.

I wish I could have been there. I would have helped them with the plans.

Daddy says our people were kings and queens in Africa. He says some of our people were poets and mathematicians, and some were artists who carved beautiful statues.

I wish I could have been there. I would have been sitting on a throne. Or maybe I would have been an artist.

Daddy says our people traveled across the ocean with Christopher Columbus and explored America with Balboa, Ponce de León, and Lewis and Clark.

I wish I could have explored new worlds with them.

Daddy says our people suffered under slavery, but men and women like Frederick Douglass, William Still, Harriet Tubman, and Sojourner Truth led our people to freedom.

I wish I could have been there. I would have led my people to freedom too.

Daddy says our people came out of slavery with nothing but hope, but that our people became anything they wanted to be. Some were politicians, some started businesses, and some became teachers and doctors. Our people farmed the land, and some went out to the wild, wild West.

I wish I could have been there. I would have gone out West too.

BLACK COWBOYS
Girls

Daddy says that our people created inventions that are still used today. He says that every time we stop at a stoplight or change a light bulb we're using something our people have invented. He says that Garrett A. Morgan, Lewis Latimer, Dr. George Washington Carver, and Dr. Charles Drew discovered some amazing scientific things to help all of humankind.

I wish I could have been there. I would have created some amazing things too.

Daddy says our people have had a glorious past, but that I have a glorious future. He says I can still build things and make beautiful things, explore new worlds, and help people who are suffering. Daddy says there are still plenty of things that need to be invented. He says I can even be a cowgirl if I want to.

I can hardly wait. I want to do something great. Just like the rest of our people.